30 SECOND
MYSTERIES

Editorial Director: Erin Conley

Designer: Lindgren/Fuller Design

Special thanks to Suzanne Cracraft and Maria Llull for their invaluable assistance!

ISBN 1-57528-907-5

CONTENTS

INTRODUCTION

Jeff Pinsker and I codeveloped dozens of games together, but none were as challenging or memorable as **30 Second Mysteries**. What a story! Jeff and I decided to invent the ultimate party game for the witty and the precocious. We wanted the game to be quick, tricky, educational, and fun. We came up with the title **30 Second Mysteries**—and the notion that if players were clever they could solve the mysteries in 30 seconds, and if we were clever we could write them in 30 seconds.

Jeff and I met one snowy day in London at the John Bull Pub to make our concept a reality. We sat for nearly nine hours and created the game as we consumed one fine British lager after another. The results of our day in London are in this volume. The **30 Second Mysteries** game was a giant success and I am now proud to present our favorite mind-bogglers in this book. I hope you have as much fun cracking the cases as we did writing them.

Bob Moog

OBJECT

To be the first player or team to solve 7 mysteries or score 7 points.

PLAYING THE GAME

• First things first: grab a pen and paper to keep track of your points.

• The youngest player spins first to determine the type of mystery to be solved (i.e. Who, What, Where, or Why) and reads the first Case and Mystery from that category out loud to the group. This player acts solely as a reader and may not play until the mystery is solved. The player to the left of the Reader gets the first clue—and the first stab at solving the mystery.

• *If a player guesses the mystery incorrectly (or doesn't have a guess)*, the player to his/her left gets the next clue and may then try to crack the case. Play proceeds in a clockwise fashion.

• *If a player guesses the mystery correctly,* s/he earns a point and the player to the Reader's left becomes the new Reader for the next case in the same category. Do not spin again until each player has read a mystery to the group.

• Once all players have acted as the Reader, it is time to spin again! The player to the left of the last person to spin now spins to determine the type of mystery to be solved. S/he is the first reader for this round.

• *Tip:* Don't forget to jot down the number of the last mystery solved in case you spin the same category more than once, which is likely to happen.

SCORING

First player to guess the mystery scores 1 point. If a player solves the mystery without hearing any clues, s/he earns 2 points.

WINNING THE GAME

The first player to score 7 points wins!

PLAYING ON YOUR OWN

Spin and read the Case and Mystery topic question from the appropriate category. Try to solve the Case using as few clues as possible.

SCORING:

6 points = 1 clue revealed
5 points = 2 clues revealed
4 points = 3 clues revealed
3 points = 4 clues revealed
2 points = 5 clues revealed
1 points = 6 clues revealed
0 points = Incorrect guess!

Read 10 mysteries. Collect 30 points or more and you're a winner!

THE CASE

A young boy arrives by train to his new school. The school is the best of its kind, but it doesn't appear on any map, nor does it appear on any list of best schools. The school is British, but is not actually in Britain. The school's fame has spread to the United States through a series of literary efforts that describe the activities of the school's unique curriculum and student body.

THE MYSTERY

What is the name of the school and who is its most famous student?

THE CLUES

The school is actually a converted castle.

The school is a boarding school that takes seven years to complete.

An owl is the school's official mascot.

The school's students don't use brooms for sweeping.

The most famous student is a seeker.

J. K. Rowling brought the school to life in her series of best-selling books.

CASE 1 SOLUTION

Harry Potter is the most famous student
at Hogwarts.

Case 2

THE CASE

A famous man has plotted the deaths of well over a hundred people, many of whom were royalty. Some survived, but many did not. The man is famous the world over for what he's done—yet he's never been tried by a court of law.

THE MYSTERY

Who are the man's two most famous victims and what is the man's name?

CLUES

The man kills his victims with his bare hands.

The man is deceased.

The man is English and lived in the 16th century.

The victims are young and their deaths are seen as a great tragedy.

The victims are star-crossed lovers.

The man knows that the pen is mightier than the sword.

CASE 2 SOLUTION

The man is William Shakespeare; his most famous victims are Romeo and Juliet.

30 SECOND
MYSTERIES

Case 3

THE CASE

In the early 1970s, a person not known as a professional athlete performs a sporting feat for the first time in recorded history. Thousands of other people would be better at performing the feat than this person, yet the media covers the event and millions of people watch.

THE MYSTERY

Who is the person and where was the sport played?

CLUES

The sport is played by millions of people.

The person is a man who works for the government.

The man is a celebrated American pilot.

The sport requires a good swing.

The sport is usually played on a course.

The man played in outer space.

CASE 3 SOLUTION

Alan B. Shepard, Jr. is an astronaut. He was the first person to play golf on the moon.

THE CASE

Despite international recognition, a well-known King never wore a crown or a robe and was not considered royalty in his native land. He was both loved and hated and could not be deterred from trying to rise up against the injustices in his land.

THE MYSTERY

Who is the man and what year did he die?

CLUES

He does not have a Roman numeral after his name.

He shares his name with his father.

The nation mourned his death.

He is a doctor, but he never went to medical school.

He died in April in Tennessee.

He was shot.

CASE 4 SOLUTION

Martin Luther King, Jr. was assassinated in Memphis in 1968.

30 SECOND MYSTERIES

WHO

Case 5

THE CASE

A person has the same job for years. The person enjoys his work, but spends most days staring at the ceiling. Despite this behavior, his work turns out to be among the most important ever done in his field.

THE MYSTERY

Who is the person and what did the person do?

CLUES

The person was left hanging for much of the job.

The person is Italian.

The job has religious overtones and could be described as "colorful."

The person was born in the 15th century.

The person is a man—and is usually known by his first name.

The man worked on the ceiling of a famous chapel.

CASE 5 SOLUTION

*Michelangelo painted the ceiling
of the Sistine Chapel.*

Case 6

THE CASE

A man spends much of his day indoors, peering through Windows. The man is not considered a recluse—rather, he has built an impressive organization, attracted a huge number of followers, and amassed great wealth. Although his organization has been under investigation by the U.S. government, many of his followers believe the man has changed their lives.

THE MYSTERY

Who is the man and what is the name of his organization?

CLUES

The man is considered a revolutionary and has followers all over the world.

The organization's materials can be found in homes throughout the U.S.

The man was born in the 1950s.

The organization is in the "hi-tech" sector.

The man is one of the wealthiest people in America.

The organization got a helping hand from IBM.

CASE 6 SOLUTION

The man is Bill Gates and the organization is Microsoft®.

---

30 SECOND MYSTERIES

WHO

Case 7

THE CASE

A masked man calmly and quietly approaches a young woman. The woman kneels and begs the masked man to leave her alone. Her husband does nothing to intervene even though he could easily stop her from being harmed. Although the masked man's identity is known, he is not arrested, even after he kills the woman.

THE MYSTERY

Who is the woman and what was her husband's name?

CLUES

The woman was 29 when she died.

The woman lived on an island.

The masked man was paid for what he did.

The woman was part of the British royal family.

The husband was the eighth in a well-known line.

The husband had many wives and ordered the woman beheaded.

CASE 7 SOLUTION

Anne Boleyn was the second wife of King Henry VIII.

30 SECOND
MYSTERIES

WHO

Case 8

THE CASE

Two men dressed in dark clothing enter a wealthy neighborhood in the early morning hours. They move quickly from house to house, taking everything they can. A policeman observes the pair—but does not approach or arrest them.

THE MYSTERY

Who are the men and what do they take?

CLUES

The men wear gloves and leave no fingerprints.

The men avoid certain houses.

The men have worked this neighborhood before and are experts at what they do.

The men aren't breaking the law.

The homeowners prepared for the men's arrival.

The men come every week at the same time.

CASE 8 SOLUTION

The men are garbage men collecting trash.

30 SECOND MYSTERIES

WHO

Case 9

THE CASE

A man with many aliases has an international reputation, but has never been seen. Occasionally, he dashes out under the cover of night. His home is very remote and nearly impossible to reach.

THE MYSTERY

What is the man called in the U.S. and where is his home?

CLUES

The man is elderly, but age doesn't slow him down.

The man's home is north of the Equator.

The man usually wears a suit.

The man has never been on a plane, but has flown all over the world.

The man employs little helpers to carry out his business.

The man's favorite pet is the reindeer.

CASE 9 SOLUTION

The man is Santa Claus and he lives
at the North Pole.

Case 10

THE CASE

With no apparent motive, a young man commits a savage attack in his neighborhood. The man's community knows about the incident, but cannot implicate him. The man's conscience eats at him until he confesses and turns himself in for punishment.

THE MYSTERY

Who is the man and what weapon did he use in his attack?

CLUES

The police were not involved and no blood appeared on the weapon.

The weapon could be held in one hand or two.

The man led many more attacks in his career.

The man went on to become a famous Father.

The weapon was used in his family's backyard.

The man has a U.S. city named after him.

CASE 10 SOLUTION

George Washington used a hatchet to chop down his family's cherry tree.

---

30 SECOND
MYSTERIES

WHO

– · – · – · – · – · –

Case 11

THE CASE

A man works with the police to identify criminals. His help is invaluable even when he hasn't witnessed the crime. Many of the criminals he identifies are never caught, but the police continue to ask the man for help. Coincidentally, the man's first name describes what he does to help the police.

THE MYSTERY

What is the man's first name and what is his occupation?

CLUES

The man's name is not unusual.

The man is on the police payroll.

The man works with his hands and listens carefully to what other people have to say.

The man is a trained professional, but also draws on his natural talent.

The man might share his name with a whole department.

The man has a three-letter name.

– · –

CASE 11 SOLUTION

The man is a police sketch artist named Art.

30 SECOND MYSTERIES

WHO

—·—·—·—·—·—·—

Case 12

THE CASE

A throng of onlookers scream when an unknown man turns on a machine. 33½ hours later, he turns the machine off and is an instant celebrity. He hasn't slept or had any visitors—but is now in a foreign country.

THE MYSTERY

Who is the man and what is his machine called?

CLUES

The man is known for being a loner.

The machine has an engine and is named for a city.

The machine hangs in the Smithsonian Institution.

The machine is an airplane.

The man became famous in 1927 and is known for his spirit.

The man was involved in a famous kidnapping.

—·—

CASE 12 SOLUTION

Charles Lindbergh's plane is
The Spirit of Saint Louis.

30 SECOND MYSTERIES

WHO

_·_·_·_·_·_·_

Case 13

THE CASE

As part of his job, a man climbs a ladder, gets caught in a windstorm, and ends up trapped inside a glass booth. Some people see him struggling and offer money; others turn their backs and walk away. The man never asks for help and no one makes any effort to help him.

THE MYSTERY

What is the man's occupation and who pays him?

CLUES

The man's job requires training.

The man wears the same outfit to work every day.

Some laugh at the man's struggles.

The man does not receive a regular paycheck.

The man relies on the kindness of strangers.

The man wears black and white makeup to work.

CASE 13 SOLUTION

The man is a mime who collects money from some of the people who watch his act.

30 SECOND
MYSTERIES

WHO

- - - - - - - - - - -

Case 14

THE CASE

A person tries for years to get the financial backing needed for a commercial venture. After finally finding a backer, the person buys materials, hires employees, and begins work. The venture doesn't meet its objective, but the person's efforts change the world and the backers are elated by the results.

THE MYSTERY

Who is the person and what year was the venture launched?

CLUES

The person is an Italian male.

The venture used existing technology in a new way.

The venture made future ventures possible.

The man's financial backers are Spanish.

The objective of the venture was to explore new territory.

The venture began near the end of the 15th century.

- -

CASE 14 SOLUTION

Christopher Columbus set sail in 1492, hoping to discover a new route to India.

30 SECOND MYSTERIES

WHO

Case 15

THE CASE

A man and his family live in a large metropolitan area. They neither own a house nor pay rent. As long as the family qualifies, they are allowed to live in housing subsidized by the government.

THE MYSTERY

Who is the family and where do they live?

CLUES

The house is in America.

The house could be called a "country" house.

The number of family members usually changes at least once a decade.

Sometimes the family has children; sometimes it doesn't.

One family member works for the government—and is a public figure.

The family lives in the nation's capital.

CASE 15 SOLUTION

The presidential family lives in the White House in Washington, D.C.

30 SECOND
MYSTERIES

Case 16

THE CASE

A man with a desk job habitually responds to emergencies. He provides his own uniform and performs these civic deeds entirely on a voluntary basis.

THE MYSTERY

Who is the man and what is on the front of his uniform?

CLUES

The man was adopted and given a new name by his parents.

The man dresses normally for work.

The man changes clothes in many different places.

The man is a journalist.

The man's uniform is primarily blue—and very well fitted.

The man can leap tall buildings in a single bound.

CASE 16 SOLUTION

---

*The man's name is Clark Kent (or Superman)
and there is an "S" on his uniform.*

---

30 SECOND MYSTERIES

WHO

Case 17

THE CASE

An extremely muscular young man in excellent health goes to bed with his girl-friend one night. When he wakes up the next morning he is still healthy, but has lost a lot of his strength. A short time later, he commits a terrorist act, taking his own life and thousands of others in the process.

THE MYSTERY

Who is the man and what was the key to his strength?

CLUES

The man kept the source of his strength secret for years.

The man's physical strength stemmed from his spiritual strength.

The man's physical appearance was altered while he slept.

The man is part of a famous pair.

The man prayed and regained his strength one last time.

The man's strength was cut short by the woman who betrayed him.

CASE 17 SOLUTION

Samson's hair was the key to his strength.

---

30 SECOND MYSTERIES

WHO

Case 18

THE CASE

One day in the late 1930s, a skillful professional goes to work and never returns home. There is no sign of foul play. The authorities conduct an extensive search, but never find the person.

THE MYSTERY

What is this person's name and profession?

CLUES

The person is a woman who was a pioneer in her profession.

The profession is still around today.

The woman was born in 1898.

The profession requires a special license.

It is presumed that the woman died, but some people are still searching for her remains today.

The woman's popularity soared to new heights after she disappeared.

CASE 18 SOLUTION

Amelia Earhart was a pilot.

THE CASE

A man meets some visitors from Africa. The visitors do not speak English, seem to be friendly, and are not wearing clothes. The visitors are in the country legally and have not committed a crime, but are behind bars. The man feels for the visitors, but does not try to help them escape.

THE MYSTERY

Who are the visitors and where are they behind bars?

CLUES

The man is in the U.S.

The visitors are behind bars for life.

The visitors make lots of noise.

The man pays to see the visitors.

The visitors are not people.

The visitors love bananas and are real "swingers."

CASE 19 SOLUTION

The visitors are monkeys in the zoo.

---

30 SECOND MYSTERIES

WHO

Case 20

THE CASE

A bald male opens his eyes and finds himself naked in a small room full of people he doesn't recognize. A female grabs him and starts to hit him before he can utter a word. He is shocked and bursts into tears.

THE MYSTERY

Who is the male and who is the female?

CLUES

The female has hit other males before.

The male is not being punished.

The female is being paid to treat the male this way.

The male is getting medical treatment.

The male has never been to a hospital before.

The male has no teeth.

CASE 20 SOLUTION

The male is a baby and the female is a doctor (obstetrician).

---

30 SECOND
MYSTERIES

WHO

Case 21

THE CASE

A man screams for over an hour and wakes up the majority of people who live in his neighborhood. Rather than complain about the noise or tell the man to stop, his neighbors give him an enthusiastic response.

THE MYSTERY

Who is the man and what four words was he yelling?

CLUES

The man is now dead.

The man was yelling for help.

The man lived near Boston, but wasn't a U.S. citizen when he yelled.

Legend has it that the man yelled the same words over and over again.

The man warned of an impending attack.

The man rode a horse and is revered as a hero.

CASE 21 SOLUTION

Paul Revere yelled, "The British are coming!"

30 SECOND
MYSTERIES

WHO

- - - - - - -

Case 22

THE CASE

A young trader travels to an exotic land where he liberates a woman and an animal. A native with a very keen sense of smell chases him—and he narrowly escapes with his life.

THE MYSTERY

Who is the trader and what did he trade in order to make his journey?

CLUES

The trader is English and never left his homeland.

The trader was inexperienced and placed his business associates' income in jeopardy.

The trader's associates were utterly disappointed with his performance and discarded his net gain.

The trader is known by his first name—and had a giant secret.

The trader speculated in bean futures.

The trader appears in a fairy tale.

- -

CASE 22 SOLUTION

Jack traded his family's cow for a handful of magic beans.

---

30 SECOND
MYSTERIES

WHO

–·–·–·–·–·–

Case 23

THE CASE

A contract is taken out on Vinnie "The Blade" Martorana. When the deal is done, Vinnie is worth more dead than alive. Vinnie knows about the contract, but does not alert the police.

THE MYSTERY

Who took out the contract and why isn't Vinnie worried?

CLUES

Vinnie knows many secrets about the person who took out the contract.

The person has a number of business arrangements with Vinnie.

Vinnie wants to live.

Vinnie has supported the person for many years.

Vinnie was in on the deal.

The person loves Vinnie and doesn't want him to die.

–·–

CASE 23 SOLUTION

Vinnie's wife took out the contract; Vinnie isn't worried because it's a life insurance contract

---

30 SECOND
MYSTERIES

WHO

–·–·–·–·–·–

Case 24

THE CASE

It was April and the sun was shining. Tens of thousands of people arrived before noon to watch the nine young men battle the monster. The uniformed employees also fought against a group of out-of-towners. While all in attendance were truly excited, they knew that they would find deep despair during the coming fall.

THE MYSTERY

Who are the employees and where are they battling the monster?

CLUES

The event took place in a New England city.

The employees were professional athletes.

The monster was green and very tall.

The young men haven't been victorious in more than 50 years of trying.

The monster lives in a Boston, Massachusetts park.

The young men played baseball.

–·–

CASE 24 SOLUTION

The employees are the Boston Red Sox. They are battling the Green Monster in Fenway Park.

THE CASE

A British subject takes a nasty tumble and is never quite the same afterwards. The subject's story is chronicled by a female poet—and becomes one of her most famous works.

THE MYSTERY

Who is the subject and what is the poet's name?

CLUES

Numerous books have been published in the poet's name.

The subject is male.

The subject cracked under pressure.

The poet is old and may never have existed.

The poet is known to be maternal.

The subject fell off a wall.

—·—

CASE 25 SOLUTION

Humpty Dumpty appears in a Mother Goose rhyme.

30 SECOND
MYSTERIES

WHO

Case 26

THE CASE

A man aboard a ship near a large city is woken up by a series of explosions. Although not in peril, the man cannot sleep and makes some notes in a journal. Years later, the notes are more important than they were during the person's lifetime.

THE MYSTERY

Who is the man and what city is closest to where he was that day?

CLUES

The words were written in the U.S.

The man was born an English citizen.

The man was anxiously awaiting sunrise.

The man's words were set to the music of an old English drinking song.

The man's song is the national anthem.

The words were written near Fort McHenry in Maryland.

CASE 26 SOLUTION

Francis Scott Key wrote the "Star Spangled Banner" near Baltimore, Maryland.

---

30 SECOND
MYSTERIES

WHO

— - — - — - — - — -

Case 27

THE CASE

A person's efforts end up inflicting pain on millions of children around the world. Despite the children's tears, the person is hailed as a hero.

THE MYSTERY

Who is the person and what resulted from the person's efforts?

CLUES

The person is a man.

The man invented a process.

The man is a doctor who lived during the 20th century.

Doctors and nurses use the process.

The process is a vaccine that cures a crippling disease.

The vaccine can now be taken orally.

— - — - — - — - — - — - — - — - — - — - — - — - — - — - — - — - — - — - — -

CASE 27 SOLUTION

Dr. Jonas Salk invented a vaccine against polio.

30 SECOND MYSTERIES

WHO

— · — · — · — · — · —

Case 28

THE CASE

Bill found himself in a dark place surrounded by a variety of precious metals. He had had a very busy day. He had started out at a suburban home, spent time in a taxi, visited a newsstand, went to a corner deli at lunchtime, and then to a movie theatre. Bill was used to change and felt like he was surrounded by it. He didn't know where he would go tomorrow, but he would probably go alone. One was, after all, Bill's favorite number.

THE MYSTERY

Who is Bill and where is he?

CLUES

People can never seem to get enough of Bill.

Bill is not a living person.

Bill sometimes gets quartered, but he never dies.

Bill is currently in a locked box surrounded by money.

Bill is made of paper.

Bill's favorite president is George Washington.

— · — · — · — · — · — · — · — · — · — · — · — · — · — · — · — · —

CASE 28 SOLUTION

---

*Bill is $1 of U.S. currency
and he is in a cash register.*

30 SECOND MYSTERIES

WHAT

‒ ‒ ‒ ‒ ‒ ‒ ‒ ‒ ‒ ‒

Case 1

THE CASE

Megan is locked in a windowless room with several dozen other people. She faces a battery of tests for nearly three hours. Megan is under intense pressure and every answer will be closely scrutinized. Her future depends on her ability to answer correctly.

THE MYSTERY

What is Megan doing, and where is she?

THE CLUE

Megan knows that her future will be affected by the test.

Megan had to show a picture ID.

Megan has been coming to this place daily for the last three years.

Megan is only 17 years old.

Megan's friends are in the room, taking the same tests.

Megan has several number #2 pencils with her—and is taking a standardized test.

‒ ‒

CASE 1 SOLUTION

Megan is taking a college entrance exam
at her high school.

30 SECOND
MYSTERIES

WHAT

— · — · — · — · — · —

Case 2

THE CASE

A huge storm gathers over the desert one January, threatening everything in its path. Thousands die and many more are injured. The storm passes, but the sky remains darkened by big black clouds.

THE MYSTERY

What two countries were most affected by the storm and what year did it hit?

THE CLUE

The storm took place in the 20th century.

The countries have a hot climate and are rich in natural resources.

The storm did not bring rain or wind.

The United States government helped create the storm.

The countries are in the Middle East.

The storm took place in the 1990s.

— · —

CASE 2 SOLUTION

Iraq and Kuwait were hit hardest by Operation Desert Storm in 1991.

Case 3

THE CASE

A steady stream of people enter Butch's place of business and remove its treasured belongings. The people do not pay for what they take. Butch allows them to take as much as they can carry as long as they keep it quiet.

THE MYSTERY

What type of business employs Butch and what are the people taking?

THE CLUE

Businesses like Butch's exist in every city in the U.S.

Butch makes sure his shelves are always stocked with merchandise.

Butch does more lending than selling.

The city government runs and owns Butch's place of business.

Sometimes Butch makes people pay when they bring the belongings back.

Butch sometimes thinks of his customers as "worms."

CASE 3 SOLUTION

Butch works for a library; people are taking books.

30 SECOND
MYSTERIES

WHAT

Case 4

THE CASE

A single man is found dead, face down in the snow, far from his home. There are no tracks around him and it has not snowed in several weeks. Hundreds of people witnessed his death, but only he could have prevented it.

THE MYSTERY

What was the man doing just before his death and how did he die?

CLUES

It was windy and cold when the man died.

The man paid to be where he was and was dressed warmly.

The man was not wearing shoes.

The man was engaged in a recreational activity.

Just before he died, the man got a real lift.

The man fell to his death.

CASE 4 SOLUTION

The man was skiing and fell off of a ski lift.

Case 5

THE CASE

A fleet of U.S. Naval vessels is heading due north into frigid Arctic waters when it comes under heavy enemy attack. One member of the flotilla sinks to the bottom and disappears from enemy radar screens. Although the captain and the entire crew went down with the ship, the rest of the fleet does not stop to look for survivors.

THE MYSTERY

What type of ship sank to the bottom and how many crew members were killed?

CLUES

The crew couldn't survive for long in the cold Arctic waters.

No crew member was found in the water.

The crew was prepared for what happened.

The ship went hundreds of feet below the surface.

The ship had sunk before.

The ship continued its voyage as planned.

CASE 5 SOLUTION

The ship is a submarine and none of the crew members were killed.

30 SECOND MYSTERIES

Case 6

THE CASE

Thousands of people attend a professional sporting event. During the event, a person drives around in a large vehicle for nearly a quarter of an hour. The driver does not count the number of laps completed and doesn't appear to be competing in any way. The spectators often appear disinterested and don't bother to cheer when the driver finishes.

THE MYSTERY

What is the vehicle's purpose and what is the event?

CLUES

The vehicle is designed for the facility where the man drives.

The event takes place indoors.

The vehicle is not part of the event.

The event has 12 active contestants.

The event is more popular in Canada than in Nevada.

The vehicle is not Italian, but its name is Zamboni®.

CASE 6 SOLUTION

The vehicle cleans the ice at ice hockey games.

30 SECOND
MYSTERIES

WHAT

- - - - - - - -

Case 7

THE CASE

Some years ago, a man left his job to travel around the world with a famous group. The group evaluated the man's credentials and told him he could not join it. The man was elated.

THE MYSTERY

What is the group's name and in what year did the man try to join?

CLUES

The year is in the 20th century.

The man is an American in his early 20s.

The group is planning a trip to Southeast Asia.

The year is one of great turmoil and the group is a source of major controversy.

The year is in the 1960s.

Uncle Sam made the man attempt to join.

- -

CASE 7 SOLUTION

The man tried to join the U.S. Army in 1969.

THE CASE

A young girl is abandoned by her family. She befriends a group of social outcasts and joins their gang. After learning of the girl's whereabouts, her family finds her and poisons her. The girl slips into a coma, but does not die.

THE MYSTERY

What is the girl's nickname and how does she survive the poisoning?

CLUES

The girl is poisoned by someone she thinks is a stranger.

The girl doesn't go by her real name.

The gang is powerless to help the girl, but keeps watch over her body.

The girl doesn't get along with her stepmother.

The gang has seven male members.

The girl is from a fairy tale and is awakened by a handsome stranger.

CASE 8 SOLUTION

Snow White survived the poisoning by getting a kiss from Prince Charming.

---

30 SECOND
MYSTERIES

– · – · – · – · – · –

Case 9

THE CASE

Wilma is working diligently in a lab when she gets a tremendous urge for a cigarette. There aren't any "No Smoking" signs posted, and the chemicals she is working with pose no real fire hazard. As soon as Wilma strikes a match, her boss fires her for destroying his work.

THE MYSTERY

In what kind of lab did Wilma work and what is her ex-boss' profession?

CLUES

Wilma is completing a specialized task.

Wilma sometimes wears gloves.

The destroyed work cannot be replaced.

Wilma's lab deals more with paper samples than blood samples.

Much of the work in the lab takes place in dim light.

Wilma's former boss is involved in the arts and has a trained eye.

– · –

CASE 9 SOLUTION

The lab is a darkroom run by Wilma's ex-boss,
who is a photographer.

---

30 SECOND MYSTERIES

WHAT

– · – · – · – · – · – · –

Case 10

THE CASE

Kim travels all over the world for free without ever buying a plane ticket or paying for lodging. She travels quickly—in some cases she visits three different continents in a single week. She works in every country that she visits, but only gets paid in one.

THE MYSTERY

What is the woman's occupation and what type of company does she work for?

CLUES

The company requires its employees to wear uniforms.

Kim is not an employee of any government.

Kim's job requires training and skills.

Kim doesn't stay long in any one place.

Kim is usually in charge when she is at work.

Kim has really taken off—and landed—in her career.

– · –

CASE 10 SOLUTION

Kim is a pilot who works for an airline.

THE CASE

Following a shipwreck in the 1960s, a group of survivors safely makes its way to an uninhabited island. The island has no food other than bananas and coconuts. The people make no real effort to farm the lands, yet they never go hungry. The survivors' plight is well known by the American public, but no rescue attempt is made.

THE MYSTERY

What is the name of the island and how many people survived the shipwreck?

CLUES

The island does not appear on any maps.

The ship was a small charter boat.

The island is known by an unofficial name.

All of the people on the ship survive the wreck.

The boat had two crewmembers and only a handful of passengers.

You can see the island from your living room.

CASE 11 SOLUTION

*The island is Gilligan's Island
and seven people survived.*

30 SECOND
MYSTERIES

WHAT

Case 12

THE CASE

During the invention of the printing press, a man publishes a book that many people already own. The book becomes an instant bestseller.

THE MYSTERY

What is the title of the book and in what century did the man publish it?

CLUES

Most people couldn't read when the book was published.

The book had two main parts.

When the man published it, the book was over 1,000 years old.

The book is still printed today.

The book changed the course of history.

The book was printed at the height of the Renaissance.

CASE 12 SOLUTION

---

*Johann Gutenberg printed a Bible
in the 15th century.*

THE CASE

An oversized rodent lives more than 60 years. Although his name, voice, and appearance change over this time period, he never appears to get any older. Employing the use of special techniques but no genetic engineering, a group of experts believes that the rodent can live forever without showing the ravages of age.

THE MYSTERY

What do the experts do for a living and what do they name the rodent?

CLUES

The experts are trained in techniques that preserve the rodent.

The experts do not practice medicine.

The rodent's first and last names start with the same letter.

The rodent's last name is descriptive.

Many of the experts are artists.

The rodent's original name was Mortimer.

CASE 13 SOLUTION

The experts are animators and
the rodent is Mickey Mouse.

30 SECOND MYSTERIES

WHAT

– · – · – · – · – · –

Case 14

THE CASE

A masked man is attacked by a gang of five men who shoot at him, then quickly flee. The masked man survives the attack, but the gang returns again and again until it finally quits. The masked man moves to a new location, but the gang continues to come after him. He moves back to his original spot, hoping in vain for a reprieve. The next night, a different gang attacks him.

THE MYSTERY

What is the masked man's profession and how long does the first set of attacks last?

CLUES

The man is protecting his turf.

The man gets shot at a lot—especially during the winter.

The gang does not fire guns.

The attacks are televised.

The man is attacked three times by the same gang in a single night for a total of 60 minutes.

The man is goal-oriented and wears a mask to protect his face.

– · – · – · – · – · – · – · – · – · – · – · – · – · – · – · – · – · – · – · –

CASE 14 SOLUTION

The masked man is a hockey goalie who is attacked for 20 minutes in the first period.

---

30 SECOND MYSTERIES

Case 15

THE CASE

An aircraft takes off and moves quickly out of sight. The aircraft doesn't use gas, wind, nuclear, or solar power—but it flies farther and faster than any craft before it.

THE MYSTERY

What is the aircraft's name and what is its power source?

CLUES

The aircraft is part of a fleet.

The aircraft usually flies for 60 minutes at a time.

An international crew flies the aircraft.

The aircraft needs special crystals to fly.

The aircraft uses a fuel based on an element with the chemical symbol "Li."

The crew and its aircraft boldly go where no other has gone before.

CASE 15 SOLUTION

Star Trek's Enterprise uses lithium crystals as fuel.

30 SECOND MYSTERIES

WHAT

Case 16

THE CASE

A man captures a wild animal and brings it back to civilization. Most days, the man leaves the animal alone and the animal ventures out on his own. The animal often gets into trouble, and the man must intervene to set things right. The man is distinguished from others by his distinctive clothing, which he appears to wear every day.

THE MYSTERY

What color clothing does the man wear and what is the animal's name?

CLUES

The man has dark hair.
You can read about the animal in books.
The animal's first name is an adjective.
The man always wears a primary color.
The man is known by the color of his hat.
The animal likes to monkey around.

CASE 16 SOLUTION

The man always wears yellow;
the animal's name is Curious George.

---

30 SECOND
MYSTERIES

— · — · — · — · — · —

Case  17

THE CASE

A man dressed in blue has a gun in one hand and a sword in the other. He fights and kills fellow citizens in a region of his country that he's never seen before. Although the country has laws against murder, he is not arrested. The man returns home—and lives the rest of his life with a clear conscience.

THE MYSTERY

What is the man's occupation and in what year did he return home?

CLUES

The man was a paid killer.

The man was lucky to survive.

The man killed in an attempt to save his country.

The man died before the turn of the century.

The man was from the North and was fighting for his country.

The man left home in 1860 and fought for five years before returning home.

— · — · — · — · — · — · — · — · — · — · — · — · — · — · — · — · —

CASE 17 SOLUTION

The man was a Union soldier who returned to his home when the Civil War ended in 1865.

30 SECOND MYSTERIES

WHAT

Case 18

THE CASE

The year is 1826. Two men who know each other well are not aware that they will both die today. While they lie near death, their life's work is being commemorated by a nation that is unaware of their conditions.

THE MYSTERY

What profession did the men share and what day did they die?

CLUES

The men died of natural causes.

The men have both been seen wearing wigs.

The date of their deaths is ironic.

The men are both American revolutionaries.

The men are Thomas Jefferson and John Adams.

Their revolution is 50 years old the day they die.

CASE 18 SOLUTION

Thomas Jefferson and John Adams were U.S. presidents who both died on July 4, 1826.

---

30 SECOND MYSTERIES

WHAT

Case 19

THE CASE

A man goes to a supermarket and buys three different products. He pays cash at the register and walks away a happy customer, realizing that he's just made a financial contribution to his favorite cause.

THE MYSTERY

What are the three products and what brand is each?

CLUES

All three products are the same brand.

All three items are edible.

The product maker is well known.

The first item is made from oil; the second is made from corn.

The man picks up the last item in the pasta isle.

The product maker is an actor who donates a portion of his proceeds to charity.

CASE 19 SOLUTION

The man bought Newman's Own Popcorn,
Pasta Sauce, and Salad Dressing.

30 SECOND
MYSTERIES

WHAT

Case 20

THE CASE

A woman is sitting outdoors and is strapped tightly into a seat. She listens nervously to a tall, well-armed man who gives her detailed instructions. After hearing what the man has to say and seeing his gun, the woman promises to follow his instructions carefully. The man lets her go.

THE MYSTERY

What does the man tell the woman to do and what type of gun persuaded her?

CLUES

The man carries one gun and has another in his car.

The woman knows she's in trouble, but doesn't fear for her life.

The man did not point either gun at the woman while he spoke.

The woman is sitting in her car on the side of the Pacific Coast Highway.

The woman will break more than a promise if she doesn't follow his instructions.

The man is a cop and pulled the woman over for speeding, but does not give her a ticket.

CASE 20 SOLUTION

The man tells her to slow down; his radar gun
clocked her speed.

---

30 SECOND MYSTERIES

WHAT

— · — · — · — · — · —

Case 21

THE CASE

Against the recommendations of her friends and family, an elderly woman begins an unusual diet. Her menu includes a wide variety of foods, but ultimately she eats something that kills her.

THE MYSTERY

What was the first item of the diet and what was the last?

CLUES

The woman is probably not real.

The woman made pet owners in her neighborhood very nervous.

By the time she ate the last item, her death was expected.

No one knows why she ate the first item.

The woman went hoarse after swallowing the last item.

The woman's diet is chronicled in a children's song and poem.

— · — · — · — · — · — · — · — · — · — · — · — · — · — · — · — · — · — · —

CASE 21 SOLUTION

The old lady swallowed a fly and
died after swallowing a horse.

---

30 SECOND
MYSTERIES

Case 22

THE CASE

It's a holiday. Moss hops into his car and begins to drive. He drives for hours in one direction and covers hundreds of miles. When Moss stops the car and gets out, he's in the same place that he started.

THE MYSTERY

In what state and in what month did Moss drive?

CLUES

Moss drives a lot and has never had a speeding ticket.

Moss planned his trip carefully.

Moss drove in this state last year at the same time.

Moss is in the midwest.

Moss drove during spring.

Moss is a professional and drives more than 100 miles per hour without getting pulled over.

CASE 22 SOLUTION

Moss drove in Indiana in May
at the Indianapolis 500.

---

30 SECOND
MYSTERIES

WHAT

_ . _ . _ . _ . _ . _

Case 23

THE CASE

In 1947, a man breaks something in California that cannot be repaired. He continues to break the thing on a regular basis, as do others. The world finds out what he has done, but takes no action against him.

THE MYSTERY

What did the man break and what type of machine did he use to break it?

CLUES

The type of machine had been around for more than 40 years when the break occurred.

The man had sound reasons for doing what he did.

The man was a captain in the Air Force.

The man passed an important barrier.

The break caused a loud explosion.

The machine traveled at a speed of 670 miles per hour.

_ . _ . _ . _ . _ . _ . _ . _ . _ . _ . _ . _ . _ . _ . _ . _ . _ . _ . _ . _

CASE 23 SOLUTION

The man (Chuck Yeager) broke the sound barrier in an airplane.

30 SECOND MYSTERIES

WHAT

Case 24

THE CASE

"OH NO! " cried the crowd. It was a cold February evening in the early 21st century and thousands of people had gathered in a remote mountain town. Millions were watching on television as the velocity of the participant increased. Like Humpty Dumpty, there was a great fall and then the hero emerged from the ground with a valuable piece of silver. "Oh no!" they cried again.

THE MYSTERY

What is the crowd doing and where are they gathered?

CLUES

The event was part of a worldwide gathering.

The participant was representing a nation.

The year was 2002.

The crowd was gathered west of the Rockies.

The participant was an American male.

The participant was speed skating.

CASE 24 SOLUTION

The crowd is watching Apolo Anton Ohno win the silver medal in the 1000-meter speed skating race at the 2002 Winter Olympics in Park City, Utah.

30 SECOND MYSTERIES

WHAT

Case 25

THE CASE

A man bets on a horse. The horse does not win a race, yet the man wins the bet. The man proves he won the bet with a process that leads to a new invention.

THE MYSTERY

What century did the bet take place and what did the invention lead to?

CLUES

The bet was not based upon speed.

Leland Stanford won the bet.

The bet was that all of a horse's hooves are off the ground at the same time.

Stanford used photographs of the horse in motion to prove he was right.

Stanford looked at each photo very quickly.

Stanford put the photos together and flipped through them quickly, in order.

CASE 25 SOLUTION

The bet took place in the late 19th century and led to the invention of the first motion picture.

THE CASE

Jason feels perfectly fit. He has no symptoms of any disease and feels no pain. After a brief exam with a doctor, Jason is told that he needs surgery. Jason has the operation and goes home bleeding profusely and in excruciating pain. The doctor declares the operation a success and tells Jason to go to work as soon as possible.

THE MYSTERY

What kind of degree does the doctor have and what did the surgery accomplish?

CLUES

The doctor studied for many years to earn her degree.

Jason won't be bothered by this problem again.

The doctor is not a MD.

The surgery is often performed on people under 30.

Jason lost four body parts during the surgery.

Surprisingly, Jason was just as smart after the operation.

CASE 26 SOLUTION

---

*The doctor has a dental degree (DDS)
and removed Jason's wisdom teeth.*

30 SECOND
MYSTERIES

WHAT

—·—·—·—·—·—·—

Case 27

THE CASE

A young woman is found dead with a large lump on the front right side of her skull. Detective Cracraft brings in nine suspects for questioning, all of whose fingerprints appear on the bloody murder weapon. He asks each suspect to fill out a number of documents. Detective Cracraft identifies the prime suspect before they complete filling out the paperwork.

THE MYSTERY

What is the murder weapon and what did Detective Cracraft notice?

CLUES

The suspects are men who know each other well.

The weapon is very popular in the U.S.

There were splinters in the dead girl's head.

All nine suspects used the weapon.

The suspects are all in uniform and work as a team.

The detective deserves a hand for his keen observation.

—·—

CASE 27 SOLUTION

The murder weapon is a baseball bat and Detective Cracraft noticed that only one suspect is left-handed.

Case 28

THE CASE

A well-known and oft-feared group of people systematically takes money from innocent men, women, and children throughout the U.S. Similar groups in other countries operate in the same organized fashion. Despite repeated public protest, the group continues its operations unabated to this day—with overt and covert help from the U.S. government.

THE MYSTERY

What is the group's name and in what century did it first appear in the U.S.?

CLUES

The group has its own code that governs its operations.

Congress passed laws specifically designed to keep the group in check.

The group takes more money now than it did when it was founded.

The group is almost as old as the U.S.

The group's annual activity peaks around April.

The group is often known by its initials.

CASE 28 SOLUTION

The group is the Internal Revenue Service,
which was founded in the 18th century.

3

WHERE

30 SECOND MYSTERIES

WHERE

Case 1

THE CASE

Years ago, two men spent every day and night together. A third man waited for them nearby. Going outside could kill the men, but they went for short walks and drives nonetheless. Now the men lead normal lives and can go outside as often as they like.

THE MYSTERY

Where were the men and what was their profession?

CLUES

The men were experts in their field.

The men's job required travel.

The men worked for the government and were selected from many applicants.

The men did not travel in a car or boat.

The men made history.

The men's careers really took off in 1969.

CASE 1 SOLUTION

The men were astronauts on the moon.

30 SECOND MYSTERIES

WHERE

—·—·—·—·—·—

Case 2

THE CASE

David is a native New Yorker. In front of thousands of witnesses, he dies a gruesome death on a busy street. At the time of his death, David is doing the same thing hundreds of other people are doing. Onlookers cheer and wave during David's demise.

THE MYSTERY

What killed David and in what country did he die?

CLUES

David did not die in the U.S.

There was no traffic on the street.

David ran for his life—but died anyway.

David died in Europe.

A herd of animals killed David.

The crowd shouted *Ole!* when David went down.

CASE 2 SOLUTION

David was trampled during the running of the bulls in Pamplona, Spain.

---

30 SECOND MYSTERIES

Case 3

THE CASE

A pane of glass separates an unknown man and a famous woman. The man stares at the woman for nearly three hours. Rather than get annoyed, the woman simply smiles back at him.

THE MYSTERY

What name is the woman commonly known by and what city is the man visiting?

CLUES

The woman has black hair and dark eyes.

The woman looks good for her age.

The man is in Western Europe's largest country.

Rumor has it that the woman looks like the second wife of Francesco.

The woman is not alive.

The man is in France looking at a painting.

CASE 3 SOLUTION

The man is looking at the Mona Lisa in Paris.

30 SECOND
MYSTERIES

- - - - - - - -

Case 4

THE CASE

People from around the world attend a series of professional sporting events, even though they know who will win. The players and referees claim that the games are not rigged and the final score does vary—but the outcome is always the same.

THE MYSTERY

Where is the winning team from and what sport do they play?

CLUES

Both men and women have played for the winning team.

The sport was invented in America, but is played all around the world.

The team's players often sport clever nicknames.

The team's players are famous for their fancy footwork.

Wilt "the Stilt" Chamberlain is one of the team's most famous players.

The team hails from the Big Apple, but has been around the globe.

- -

CASE 4 SOLUTION

The Harlem Globetrotters play basketball.

30 SECOND MYSTERIES

Case 5

THE CASE

A man walks to a place where nothing will happen for several hours. He stands in a city square with thousands of other people—many of whom are speaking foreign languages. The man checks his watch regularly and looks upward in nervous anticipation.

THE MYSTERY

Where is the man and what is he waiting for?

THE CLUES

The man is in the United States.

Camera crews are standing by.

The man is waiting for something to begin—and to end.

The man is on Broadway, but is not a performer.

The man receives several kisses from strangers.

The man is expecting fireworks, but it's not July.

CASE 5 SOLUTION

It's New Year's Eve and the man is in New York's Times Square waiting for midnight.

30 SECOND MYSTERIES

Case 6

THE CASE

A group of people stumbles across a body. After examining the corpse, the group notes that the body is missing internal organs—but maintains the victim died a natural death.

THE MYSTERY

What is the people's occupation and in what country did they find the body?

CLUES

The people have no medical training.

The country is north of the Equator.

Some of the people are doctors.

The country is in Northern Africa.

The country is home to King Tut.

The people really dig their job.

CASE 6 SOLUTION

The people are archaeologists working in Egypt.
(They uncovered a mummy.)

---

30 SECOND MYSTERIES

WHERE

—·—·—·—·—·—

Case 7

THE CASE

A man's body is found 1,000 feet below sea level. Drowning is not the cause of death.

THE MYSTERY

Where and how did the man die?

CLUES

The man died north of the Equator.

The man died of "natural causes," but many things could have killed him.

The man died face down.

The man died in a U.S. desert.

The sun was out when the man died.

The man died in a California valley known for its killer heat.

—·—

CASE 7 SOLUTION

The man died of heat exhaustion in Death Valley.

30 SECOND MYSTERIES

WHERE

- - - - - - - -

Case 8

THE CASE

A man with a large collection of knives skillfully dismembers his victims in a precise manner. The police know where the man lives and where he disposes of the dismembered parts, but never question or arrest him.

THE MYSTERY

Where does the man dispose of his victims and what is the man's profession?

CLUES

The man could be in any town in the U.S.

The man rarely sees his victims before they die.

The man is a paid professional.

The man works indoors and wears white.

The man dumps his victims in a large metal container behind his place of business.

The man really knows his meat.

- -

CASE 8 SOLUTION

The man is a butcher; he disposes of his victims in the dumpster behind his meat market.

THE CASE

A man enters a sweepstakes one summer and is notified by mail that he has won third prize: a new refrigerator. The man owns his home, but does not have a fridge. Although there are no hidden costs and he needs to keep his family's food cold, the man turns down the prize.

THE MYSTERY

What is the man's home called and in what U.S. state does he live?

CLUES

The man's home is similar to his closest neighbors' homes.

The man's home borders the Pacific.

The man is a fisherman who built his house by himself.

The house is on land and is made from unusual building materials.

The man lives in the largest U.S. state.

The man's home is round.

—·—

CASE 9 SOLUTION

The man lives in an igloo in Alaska.

Case 10

THE CASE

Ben has a high profile and an easily recognizable face. Ben's home sits near water, but has been attacked many times by land. Security guards protect his home 24 hours a day, while Ben entertains visitors, poses for pictures, and goes about his business with no worries.

THE MYSTERY

What service does Ben provide and what city is Ben's home?

CLUES

Ben depends on his hands and face.

Ben lives on an island.

Ben's service requires punctuality.

Ben is big in his field.

Ben's city was attacked in World War II, but he survived.

Ben's city is part of Europe and is the capital of its country.

CASE 10 SOLUTION

(Big) Ben tells time in London.

Case 11

THE CASE

A group of men take care of a large number of horses near the ocean. Every summer, adults come from miles around to watch the horses. The horses run during the day and late at night, stopping only for short breaks. The men never feed the horses, even though the horses are their sole source of income.

THE MYSTERY

Where are the horses kept and what type of horses are they?

CLUES

The men live north of the equator and east of the mighty Mississippi.

The horses never stray far from their home and always follow the same path.

The horses have endured for many years.

The horses are found on the Eastern Seaboard.

Riding the horses can have its ups and downs.

The horses are kept on a New York island—famous for its hot dogs.

CASE 11 SOLUTION

The horses are Coney Island carousel horses.

30 SECOND MYSTERIES

WHERE

— · — · — · — · — · — · —

Case 12

THE CASE

Hundreds of people visit Jim every week. The people respect Jim, but tend to walk all over him. Jim offers no objection and never complains about his visitors.

THE MYSTERY

What is Jim's last name and in what city does he reside?

CLUES

Jim is an American.

Everyone who visits knows Jim's last name.

Jim hasn't moved since 1971.

Jim is best known for his music.

Tragically, Jim's flame burned out at age 27.

Jim is buried in a French cemetery.

— · —

CASE 12 SOLUTION

Jim's last name is Morrison, and he resides in Paris.

30 SECOND MYSTERIES

WHERE

—·—·—·—·—·—

Case 13

THE CASE

A man builds a fortified structure to keep out his neighbors, but dies before it's completed. By the time his successors finish the structure, it is so large that it can be seen from outer space.

THE MYSTERY

In what country was the structure built and what is it called?

CLUES

The structure is north of the Equator.

The structure took centuries to complete.

Building started in the 3rd century B.C.

The structure takes its name from its country and is part of a dynasty's legacy.

The structure's average height is 25 feet and it is more than 1,500 miles long.

The structure is a popular Chinese tourist destination.

—·—

CASE 13 SOLUTION

The Great Wall of China was built
in China and is a wall.

30 SECOND MYSTERIES

WHERE

Case 14

THE CASE

After years of bloody war on a scale greater than anything in recorded history, one side unveils a secret weapon—and uses it. Many lives are lost and the other side quickly surrenders.

THE MYSTERY

Where was the weapon unleashed and what was the weapon?

CLUES

The weapon was unleashed on a major city.

The weapon was unleashed in Asia near the Dardanelles.

From the outside, the weapon looked harmless.

The weapon was pulled inside the city's walls.

The weapon was a large four-legged animal made of wood.

A woman named Helen had a lot to do with the conflict.

CASE 14 SOLUTION

The Trojan Horse was unleashed on the city of Troy.

30 SECOND
MYSTERIES

WHERE

–·–·–·–·–·–

Case 15

THE CASE

A Danish woman travels to Africa in the middle of summer with a group of friends. One night, the group pitches its tent less than 200 miles from the Equator. The next morning, the woman and her entire party are found frozen to death.

THE MYSTERY

In what country was the group camping and where did they pitch their tent?

CLUES

The country borders the Indian Ocean.

The group complained about the jungle heat one day before they died.

The group wasn't prepared for the cold.

The group was at a high altitude.

The country borders Kenya and is home to the Serengeti National Park.

The group was atop Africa's highest mountain.

–·–

CASE 15 SOLUTION

*The group was camping in Tanzania
atop Mount Kilimanjaro.*

30 SECOND
MYSTERIES

Case 16

THE CASE

A man goes out drinking every night and doesn't come home until the wee hours of the morning. No matter how much he drinks the night before, the man never has a hangover.

THE MYSTERY

Where is the man's home and what is his favorite drink?

CLUES

The man lives north of the Equator.

The man is a sucker for a free drink.

The man lives alone in a European castle.

The man gets his drink straight from the source.

The man lives in a well-known region of Hungary.

The man always has a quick bite before he has a drink.

CASE 16 SOLUTION

The man is a vampire who lives in Transylvania and drinks blood.

Case 17

THE CASE

A group of four comes together and follows a road they believe will lead to enlightenment. The group's leader brings along a trusted companion.

THE MYSTERY

What is the name of the leader's companion and in what city does the road end?

CLUES

All four members of the group sing.

You won't find the city on any map.

There are no signs on the road.

The leader's companion has four legs.

The city is named after a precious gem and the road is made of brick.

The leader and her four-legged friend aren't in Kansas anymore.

CASE 17 SOLUTION

The animal's name is Toto and the road ends at the Emerald City.

THE CASE

An elderly woman is walking down the sidewalk of a busy city street when she suddenly falls to the ground and dies. The authorities search for her body, but don't find it for nearly five days—even though it was on the sidewalk the entire time.

THE MYSTERY

In what city did the woman die and why couldn't her body be found?

CLUES

The woman was 80 years old in 1900.

The woman's age had nothing to do with her fall.

The woman did not die from the fall.

Just before she died, the woman admired a bay in the Pacific Ocean.

The woman was headed down a steep hill.

Something fell on the woman during a natural disaster.

CASE 18 SOLUTION

The woman died in the San Francisco earthquake; her body was covered by rubble for five days.

30 SECOND
MYSTERIES

WHERE

Case 19

THE CASE

A group of famous people hangs out together every day—though some have never even met each other. Many people have seen them together, but if asked, no one in the group would acknowledge that they've had a blast together.

THE MYSTERY

What are the people's last names and where can the people be seen together?

CLUES

There are four men in the group.

The men are in the U.S.

People look up to the men—literally.

The men are from different time periods.

The men are all American heads of state.

The men can be found in the Black Hills of South Dakota.

CASE 19 SOLUTION

---

*The men are Washington, Jefferson, Lincoln,
and Roosevelt; they can be seen together
at Mount Rushmore.*

---

30 SECOND MYSTERIES

WHERE

_ . _ . _ . _ . _ . _

Case 20

THE CASE

A woman is accused of a crime, tried in an American court of law, and found guilty. The woman has not killed anyone or committed treason, yet the judge orders the death penalty. Her execution is swift and there is no appeal or public protest.

THE MYSTERY

What crime was the woman convicted of and in what town was she executed?

CLUES

The town is part of a British colony.

18 other people died for the same crime.

The town is on the East Coast of the U.S.

The crime is no longer tried in U.S. courts.

Frank Sinatra crooned about the crime the woman allegedly committed.

The conviction was in Massachusetts in 1692.

_ . _

CASE 20 SOLUTION

*The woman was convicted of witchcraft
in Salem, Massachusetts.*

30 SECOND MYSTERIES

WHERE

Case 21

THE CASE

Late one evening, a young couple gets into a car. The man presses his foot to the floor and the car accelerates through the darkness until it suddenly plunges hundreds of feet, flips over, and comes to rest. The young couple get out of the car quickly, shaken but unscathed.

THE MYSTERY

Where was the couple and what type of car were they in?

CLUES

The couple is on vacation.

The couple paid to use the car.

The young man is not the driver.

The couple is in California and is surrounded by lots of people.

The car is attached to other cars.

Just before getting into the car, the couple saw a mouse.

CASE 21 SOLUTION

The couple was in a roller coaster car at Disneyland.

THE CASE

A person witnesses a string of shootings while working in a foreign country during the 1970s, but makes no effort to stop them. After telling others about the incidents, the person wins a prize that rewards "courage and honesty."

THE MYSTERY

What is the person's occupation and in what country were the shootings?

CLUES

The person does not work for the police.

The country is just north of the Equator.

The person needed official permission to do his job.

The country borders the South China Sea.

The person is a paid informer, but is not a spy.

The country was a war zone for many years.

CASE 22 SOLUTION

The person is a journalist in Vietnam.

THE CASE

Julio is an American citizen born in 1956. He has never been out of the country, nor has he entered a single U.S. state.

THE MYSTERY

Where does Julio live and what two states are closest to his home?

CLUES

Julio is often surrounded by foreigners.

Julio works and pays taxes to the IRS.

Both states are south of the Mason-Dixon line.

Julio can take public transit to the two states closest to his home.

Both states are smaller because of the place where Julio lives.

Julio lives in a capital city on the U.S. mainland.

CASE 23 SOLUTION

Julio lives in Washington D.C.; Maryland and Virginia are the closest states to his home.

THE CASE

On February 9, Joseph celebrates his 30th birthday with friends and family. At noon, he packs up his belongings, boards a plane, and leaves his native land forever. After a five hour flight he gets off the plane—and realizes it's no longer his birthday.

THE MYSTERY

What country did Joseph leave and how many days away is his next birthday?

CLUES

Joseph does not speak English as a native language.

Joseph reset his watch while en route.

Joseph traveled between two large countries and flew in an easterly direction.

Joseph is officially 29 when he lands and will celebrate his 30th birthday a second time.

Chronologically, Joseph arrived before he left.

Joseph drove past the Kremlin on his way to the airport.

—·—

CASE 24 SOLUTION

Joseph left Russia; his birthday is one day away.
(He crossed the International Date Line.)

Case 25

THE CASE

Hughes Bank has just been robbed! Two miles from the bank, Lydia is racing down the highway. She has not committed a crime, but three police cars are hot on her trail. Lydia does not pull over—and continues to speed through traffic with the police following her every move.

THE MYSTERY

Where is Lydia heading and what is her profession?

CLUES

Lydia has never been to her destination before.

Lydia knows about the robbery.

Lydia will continue at top speed until she reaches her destination.

Lydia carries a revolver—and won't hesitate to use it.

The police will tail Lydia all the way to her destination.

Lydia does not own the car she's driving and is about to become involved in the robbery.

CASE 25 SOLUTION

Lydia is a police officer heading toward Hughes Bank.

Case 26

THE CASE

In 1996, a boat carrying an object of extreme international importance lands in San Francisco. Upon landing, a lone man grabs the object and starts to run. Some miles away, he passes it off to a woman, who continues running in the same direction. The object is carried to its destination, where it remains for some time before starting the process again.

THE MYSTERY

What is the object and what city was its destination?

CLUES

The city is in the U.S.

The item is relatively light.

The city is south of New York and east of the Mississippi.

The item has been more or less in motion since it was first created and is instantly recognizable.

The item starts a fire every four years and is an international symbol.

The city is in Georgia.

CASE 26 SOLUTION

The Olympic Torch was on its way to Atlanta.

Case 27

THE CASE

A woman whose husband has just left her lets out an anguished cry and leaps off a tall cliff overlooking the ocean. The woman survives the fall—without even getting wet.

THE MYSTERY

Where did the woman land and how did the woman survive?

CLUES

The woman landed on a surface hard enough to kill her.

The woman was not prepared to die, but was prepared to jump.

The woman did not have a parachute.

The woman did not land in the ocean.

The woman picked her landing spot before she jumped.

The woman glided to the ground.

CASE 27 SOLUTION

*The woman had a hang glider
and landed on the beach.*

Case 28

THE CASE

A boy walks into a building and stands in a line. When he gets to the front of the line he discusses his current desires with a uniformed employee of the establishment. He waits 1–2 minutes, pays $1.99 and then departs with a white bag. His expression matches the name of the product he has just purchased.

THE MYSTERY

Where is the boy and what did he purchase?

CLUES

The building shares its name with a famous American farmer.

The boy is happy.

The boy received a toy with his purchase.

The boy is not a vegetarian.

The building is similar to a thousand other similar buildings.

The boy associates the place with a guy named Ronald.

—·—

CASE 28 SOLUTION

*The boy is in McDonald's and
he purchased a Happy Meal.*

THE CASE

A woman in Fresno, California gets on a bus heading east. She has only $10 in her pocket, but dreams of seeing the Empire State Building. After less than 10 hours, the woman gets off the bus and waves goodbye to the other passengers. She gives the man at the counter a dollar and asks him for change. Twenty minutes later the woman looks up at the Empire State Building and smiles.

THE MYSTERY

Why does the woman ask for change and what city is she in?

THE CLUES

The woman is no longer in California.

The weather is pleasant, but the woman chooses to spend most of her time indoors.

The city is full of tourists.

The man gave the woman four quarters for a dollar.

The woman spotted Elvis on the way to the Empire State building.

The woman plans to see the Hoover Dam later in the day.

CASE 1 SOLUTION

---

*The woman is in Las Vegas and needs change
to play the slot machines.*

---

30 SECOND
MYSTERIES

WHY

— · — · — · — · — · — · —

Case 2

THE CASE

It's the first day of spring and a group of photographers gather in a garden full of colorful blooms. Despite the beautiful flowers surrounding them, the photographers focus on four Bushes strategically placed on the lawn. The Bushes are not in bloom, have no visible roots and are of various sizes and ages.

THE MYSTERY

What garden are the photographers in and why are they interested in these particular Bushes?

CLUES

The garden is in the United States.

The Bushes come from the same family and species.

The flowers in bloom are roses.

Other Bushes in the same family have been photographed here before.

The garden is located at 100 Pennsylvania Avenue.

The Bushes came from Texas—and have deep roots in politics.

— · — · — · — · — · — · — · — · — · — · — · — · — · — · — · — · — · — · — · — ·

CASE 2 SOLUTION

The photographers are in the White House Rose Garden to take pictures of George W. Bush and family.

THE CASE

A man is fishing on a small, peaceful lake in a remote area of North America. While enjoying the sunshine, he accidentally falls into the water. The man is a former Olympic swimmer, but he is unable to swim the 50 yards to shore. Although he keeps his head above water and doesn't drown, he dies within 30 minutes.

THE MYSTERY

Why couldn't the man swim to shore and what was the cause of death?

CLUES

The man was in top physical condition.

The man was conscious when he fell into the water.

No one heard the man call for help.

The man was wearing a lot of clothes.

Conditions on the lake prevented the man from swimming.

The man had been ice skating on the lake the day before.

CASE 3 SOLUTION

The man died of hypothermia and couldn't swim because the lake was covered with ice.

30 SECOND MYSTERIES

Case 4

THE CASE

Jules is the guest of honor at a party. He downs seven drinks in a three-hour period. Despite warnings from his friends, Jules runs outside, hops into the bright red Ferrari parked in the driveway and drives away. Minutes later, he crashes into a tree and totals the car. The police administer a blood-alcohol test and find no alcohol in Jules' bloodstream.

THE MYSTERY

Why were the test results negative and why did Jules have the accident?

CLUES

The accident occurred at night on July 4, 2001.

Jules was indulging in his favorite drink.

Jules was not a good driver, but had never received a ticket.

The test results were accurate, but Jules did break the law.

Jules' drink of choice is carbonated and likely to give him a sugar high.

Jules was born on October 4, 1987.

CASE 4 SOLUTION

Jules was drinking soda, but he was only 15 years old and didn't know how to drive.

---

30 SECOND MYSTERIES

Case 5

THE CASE

Sue is an accomplished sculptor. She crafts beautiful pieces that weigh hundreds of pounds and carefully delivers them to her clients. Within 24 hours of delivery, every sculpture disappears. Sue does not seem to be upset by these disappearances.

THE MYSTERY

Why isn't Sue upset and what happens to the sculptures?

CLUES

The sculptures haven't been stolen.

Sue must work quickly.

Everyone agrees that Sue's sculptures are cool.

You won't find the sculptures in a museum.

The sculptures are made from a common material, and are heat sensitive.

Sue uses a chain saw and gloves while working.

CASE 5 SOLUTION

Sue is an ice sculptor; her sculptures melt.

30 SECOND
MYSTERIES

WHY

— · — · — · — · — · —

Case 6

THE CASE

A man from Chicago deliberately puts on shorts and a tank top, then goes outside in the middle of winter and walks along a lake. The wind is blowing and it's 20° outside, but the man is delighted that he's not bundled up for the winter like the rest of the residents of Chicago.

THE MYSTERY

Why can the man tolerate the weather and what is he doing?

CLUES

The man is quite comfortable and, from a physical standpoint, is quite average.

The man has saved a lot of money to engage in this activity.

The man's wife is dressed in a similar fashion.

The man is far from his work and home.

The man was recently a passenger on an airplane.

The forecast predicts that the weather will be molto caldo oggi.

— · —

CASE 6 SOLUTION

The man is on vacation where the temperature is 20° Celsius.

30 SECOND MYSTERIES

WHY

–·–·–·–·–·–

Case 7

THE CASE

Bob and Ursula are having an intense conversation while Bob is trying to concentrate on driving their two-seater sports car down a winding mountainous road. Bob has a seat belt on, but Ursula does not. Suddenly, a truck swerves and hits their car head on. Their car is totaled, with equal damage on the driver's side and the passenger's side. Bob has two broken legs and a broken pelvis, but Ursula doesn't have a scratch on her body. Ursula calls the police right away, but can't tell them where the accident happened.

THE MYSTERY

Why isn't Ursula injured and why doesn't she know where the accident occurred?

CLUES

Ursula usually wears her seat belt.

Ursula was not wearing any special protection.

Ursula was not disoriented by the impact of the crash and was not thrown from the car.

Ursula has a good sense of direction and good vision, but she never saw the other car coming.

Ursula could hear Bob but couldn't see him.

Ursula was not close to the scene of the accident.

–·–

CASE 7 SOLUTION

Ursula was not in the car; she was talking to Bob on his cell phone.

30 SECOND
MYSTERIES

WHY

—·—·—·—·—·—

Case 8

THE CASE

An elderly woman goes for a leisurely walk. Two young men in excellent physical condition are directly behind her, sprinting toward her. No matter how fast they run, they do not catch up with the woman.

THE MYSTERY

Why can't the men catch up with the woman and where are all three people?

CLUES

The men are running as fast as they can.

There are other people in the same area.

The men always stay seven feet behind the woman.

All three people paid money to be where they are.

The men are not moving forward.

All three people are indoors.

—·—

CASE 8 SOLUTION

All three people are on treadmills in a gym.

Case 9

THE CASE

A group of uniformed men calmly and methodically enters a house during broad daylight and takes every possession that a family owns. The family does not contact the police, but does find their belongings three days later.

THE MYSTERY

Why weren't the authorities involved and where did the family find their belongings?

CLUES

The family knows how the men operate.

The men are not part of any government agency.

The men are known for taking things.

The family found their belongings in a different city.

The belongings were exactly where the family expected them to be.

The family gave the men money, but it was not a ransom for their belongings.

CASE 9 SOLUTION

The men are movers and the family found their belongings in their new house.

---

30 SECOND MYSTERIES

WHY

Case 10

THE CASE

A drunken man leaves his favorite bar at midnight and starts stumbling toward his home. By the light of a full moon, he decides to take a shortcut. Along the way, he trips, hits his head on a rock and passes out. He never regains consciousness and is dead by morning. Although his footprints are visible, his body is never found.

THE MYSTERY

Why is the man's body never found and how did he die?

CLUES

The man did not die of alcohol poisoning.

The man was reported as missing.

The fall did not kill the man, but it did knock him unconscious.

The man's body was moved from the spot where he fell—but not by people.

The man lived on the beach in Hawaii.

The man died at high tide.

CASE 10 SOLUTION

*The man drowned and the body
was washed out to sea.*

30 SECOND
MYSTERIES

WHY

—·—·—·—·—·—·—

Case 11

THE CASE

Chip is never allowed to leave his home alone, even though he is middle aged.
When he leaves his home, under strict supervision, thousands of people come to
watch him. Chip is in excellent health and has no known mental problems. He
is well cared for and never complains about his restrictive living arrangements.

THE MYSTERY

Why doesn't Chip complain and what is his profession?

CLUES

Chip is a professional, yet earns no money for himself.
Although Chip could survive in the outside world, he would lose his job.
Chip is an athlete who follows his instincts when he competes.
Even when he's out in front, Chip is a follower, not a leader.
Chip only eats special food.
Chip loves to go to the races.

—·—

CASE 11 SOLUTION

Chip is a dog who competes in dog races.

30 SECOND MYSTERIES

WHY

Case 12

THE CASE

A woman is sitting in an easy chair reading a book when a masked man bursts into her room and snatches her purse. Although the man carries no weapon and was less than 6 feet from the woman, she makes no effort to stop him. She reports the crime to the police and provides a description of her purse, but gives no details about the masked man.

THE MYSTERY

Why didn't the woman describe the masked man and in what language is her book written?

CLUES

The woman did not know the man, but she knew the man was breaking into her home.

The woman was reading War and Peace, by a Russian writer named Tolstoy.

The woman only speaks English.

The man knew only one thing about the woman.

The woman did not see the man.

The woman's hands were busy at the time of the break-in.

CASE 12 SOLUTION

The woman is blind and was reading a book in Braille.

30 SECOND MYSTERIES

WHY

–·–·–·–·–·–

Case 13

THE CASE

With pounding hearts, six women take off running when they hear a gunshot. Without even a second glance at the women, the man with the gun calmly lowers the still-smoking revolver and walks away. He does not fire another shot, but makes no attempt to flee. The entire scene is captured by live TV news cameras, but no arrest is made.

THE MYSTERY

Why did the man shoot and how far away from the man did the women run?

CLUES

The man shoots guns on a regular basis.

The man does not know any of the women personally.

The women were expecting to hear a shot.

The women ran as fast as they could without looking back until they reached a barrier.

The man is paid to shoot, but he's never hit anyone.

The women ran for less than 12 seconds.

–·–

CASE 13 SOLUTION

The man is a starter in the Olympics and the women ran 100 meters.

Case 14

THE CASE

Dr. Cooper, a registered surgeon, goes into surgery and immediately passes out. The operation is finished by the time that Dr. Cooper comes to. After a physical and a night's rest, he is called upon to perform an operation on a young child. Even though the hospital authorities know that the patient will die if Dr. Cooper passes out again, no other surgeons are present.

THE MYSTERY

Why did Dr. Cooper pass out and why is he trusted to perform the operation on the child?

CLUES

Dr. Cooper is an experienced surgeon.

Dr. Cooper's operation was a success.

Dr. Cooper has never passed out before and there is no reason to believe that Dr. Cooper will pass out again.

It did not surprise anyone that Dr. Cooper passed out.

Even after Dr. Cooper passed out, the initial operation could not have proceeded without him.

Dr. Cooper was not operating when he passed out.

CASE 14 SOLUTION

Dr. Cooper passed out because he was given anesthesia; he can operate now that he is recovered from his surgery.

30 SECOND MYSTERIES

WHY

Case 15

THE CASE

In addition to pictures of his wife and children, Peter Cannon carries pictures of a number of dead people with him at all times. Peter admires the people, but they are not members of his family. Even though some of the pictures are extremely valuable, Peter often gives them away.

THE MYSTERY

Why does Peter carry the pictures and why does he give them away?

CLUES

The people in the pictures are famous and he gives some away every day.
Peter is not part of any religious cult.
The fewer number of pictures that Peter gives away, the better he feels.
The pictures are wallet-sized and were not taken with a camera.
Peter trades the pictures for things that he wants.
Peter once had a picture of Grover Cleveland; it was his favorite.

CASE 15 SOLUTION

Peter carries pictures because they are printed on money, which he gives away when he buys things.

30 SECOND MYSTERIES

WHY

Case 16

THE CASE

A scuba diver is 1,000 feet below the surface when the oxygen in his tank runs out. The diver doesn't make it to the surface for nearly three hours, yet he doesn't die when his oxygen runs out.

THE MYSTERY

Why didn't the diver die when his oxygen ran out and how did he reach the surface?

CLUES

The man was an experienced diver.

The diver didn't know that his oxygen supply had been exhausted.

The man's training did not help him reach the surface.

It was impossible for the diver to die from lack of air.

The diver did not reach the surface under his own power.

The diver died from a heart attack.

CASE 16 SOLUTION

The diver was already dead when his oxygen ran out and his body floated up to the surface.

THE CASE

Bob is a government employee who spends his entire work day sitting down. His customers pay money and watch him sit. Bob ignores these customers while he looks outside through his office window. If Bob does his job correctly, the customers leave as soon as he is finished.

THE MYSTERY

Why do the customers leave and what is Bob's job?

CLUES

The customers keep moving all the time they're with Bob.

Bob wears a uniform while he works.

Bob works for the city and has a great view of the city.

The customers sit while they are with Bob.

When the customers leave Bob they are on the street.

Bob drives a vehicle.

—·—

CASE 17 SOLUTION

Bob is a bus driver; the customers leave when they reach their stops.

Case 18

THE CASE

Jack Jensen is an All-Star baseball player near the end of an illustrious career in which he broke numerous records. He's been a starting player since he broke into the majors, and he's never been pulled for a pinch hitter. In his final game, played at the opponent's stadium, Jensen earns a huge ovation from the crowd as he steps up to the plate for the first time ever.

THE MYSTERY

Why hasn't Jensen hit before and what month is it?

CLUES

Jensen was a decent hitter in college and has shown up for batting practice for his entire career.

Jensen comes to the plate during the U.S.'s professional baseball season.

Jensen's team has lost more games than it won for the past 11 years, but has finally had a winning season.

Jensen handles the ball on every play when he's on the field and his hitting is a sign of his team's success.

Jensen has never played baseball in this month before.

The game is played in St. Louis, Missouri.

CASE 18 SOLUTION

It's October and Jensen is a pitcher in the American League playing in the World Series.

---

30 SECOND MYSTERIES

WHY

—·—·—·—·—·—

Case 19

THE CASE

Just before closing time, a group of heavily armed men jump out of a vehicle and cautiously enter a bank. One man stays with the vehicle and keeps the motor running. The group's leader approaches a teller and hands her a note. The teller opens the vault and the men take tens of thousands of dollars. Even after the men are gone, the teller does not trip the alarm.

THE MYSTERY

Why doesn't the teller trip the alarm and what type of vehicle are the men driving?

CLUES

The vehicle is designed for quick get-aways.

The teller has seen the men before.

The teller was in on the job, but committed no crime.

The vehicle heads for another bank.

The vehicle is well-marked.

Although its official name is a car, the vehicle is a truck.

—·—

CASE 19 SOLUTION

The men are security guards who
are driving an armored car.

---

30 SECOND MYSTERIES

WHY

Case 20

THE CASE

Jill Svoboda is driven from her home in Los Angeles, California to a government building. She meets an official who travels with her for a time, then directs her back to the building. At the building, Jill is fingerprinted and photographed, even though she has committed no crime. Jill drives home with a smile on her face.

THE MYSTERY

Why was Jill smiling and what agency does the official work for?

CLUES

The official works for the state.

This is the first time Jill has done this.

The official spends most of his time on the road.

No one speeds when they are with the official, but the official is not a police officer.

Jill breathed a sigh of relief just before she started smiling.

Jill is only 16 years old and spent months preparing for her visit to the building.

CASE 20 SOLUTION

The official works for the Department of Motor Vehicles; Jill is smiling because she just passed her driving test.

THE CASE

With painstaking attention to detail, Candy writes down all the lurid, juicy specifics of a crime. She is not a police officer, but she wears a uniform. Candy follows every word spoken with great interest, but she isn't involved with anyone in the trial and has no vested interest in the outcome.

THE MYSTERY

Why does Candy follow the crime and what does she do for a living?

CLUES

Candy has followed crimes like this before.

Candy is not a journalist or a law student.

Candy has no opinion on the crime.

Candy is paid to follow the crime.

Candy works for the court.

Candy is sitting on a bench and is wearing a robe.

CASE 21 SOLUTION

Candy is a judge presiding over a trial.

30 SECOND
MYSTERIES

WHY

_._._._._._._

Case 22

THE CASE

Nina and Maia are making a fortune in real estate. Even though Nina never breaks the law, she is sent to jail. Maia follows the same procedures as Nina with many of the same properties, but she never goes to jail.

THE MYSTERY

Why did Nina go to jail and what is the maximum amount of time she could spend there?

CLUES

Nina has been in jail before.

Nina never had a trial before she was instructed to go to jail.

Nina's sentence is the same for others in her circumstance.

Nina never leaves her home when she goes to jail.

Nina didn't collect any money on her way to jail.

Nina needs a good roll—not parole.

_._

CASE 22 SOLUTION

Nina is playing Monopoly® and landed on the square that says "Go to Jail." She could spend up to three turns there.

30 SECOND MYSTERIES

WHY

— · — · — · — ·

Case 23

THE CASE

In 1994, a man's dead body is found, sitting upright, in a small room with no windows. Had the year been 1989, he would not have died. Even before the authorities open the door, they know that the man did not take his own life.

THE MYSTERY

How did the man die and why wouldn't he have died in 1989?

CLUES

The man didn't want to die.

The man died in California.

The man knew he was going to die.

The man's death was very controversial.

The man had a troubled past.

The man died because something changed between 1989 and 1994.

— · — · — · — · — · — · — · — · — · — · — · — · — · — · — · — · — · — · —

CASE 23 SOLUTION

The man died of electrocution because the death penalty was legalized in California.

THE CASE

In the 1950s, a doctor prescribes an unusual—and unappetizing—diet to a relectant individual. The doctor never talks to the individual about his case, but publishes the diet in a best selling book.

THE MYSTERY

Why did the doctor create the diet and what is the title of his book?

CLUES

The doctor holds no medical degree, but hopes the public will buy his
   diet anyway.

The reluctant individual is known only by his first name.

The doctor has also written about cats, turtles, and fish.

The doctor's given name is Theodore Geisel.

The reluctant individual goes by the name of Sam.

The meal consists of meat and a discolored dairy product.

CASE 24 SOLUTION

The doctor, Dr. Seuss, created the diet to sell books!
The book is Green Eggs and Ham.

Case 25

THE CASE

"Lucky" Jim is a world-class runner. While the world looks on, Jim wins his most important race, but trips and falls just past the finish line. Jim is quickly rushed away in an ambulance. The next day, a man shoots and kills him. Given Jim's fame, his death was front-page news. Although the authorities know who killed Jim, they make no effort to arrest or charge the killer.

THE MYSTERY

Why wasn't Jim's killer charged with murder and what race did Jim win?

CLUES

Jim's death was expected.

Jim's killer did not break any laws.

Jim ran after racing a distance of 1½ miles.

Jim broke his leg in the fall.

Jim's killer is a doctor who practices in Belmont, New York.

Jim is less than four years old.

CASE 25 SOLUTION

Jim won the Belmont Stakes, and his killer was a veterinarian.

THE CASE

In the midst of war, a king captures a queen and is then, in turn, captured. The captor is not in the military, but does hold a specific rank. All three survive to do battle again, and the circumstances are repeated. In fact, each time that they are face to face, there is no way that any other outcome is possible.

THE MYSTERY

Why is no one injured and what rank captures the king?

CLUES

The captor does not wear a uniform.

The war is popular.

The war is waged by common people and may even involve children.

The king was captured by a rank just above him.

Like the king, the captor is a real card.

No weapons were used in this war.

— · — · — · — · — · — · — · — · — · — · — · — · — · — · — · — · — · —

CASE 26 SOLUTION

An ace captures the king; no one is injured because war is just a card game!

THE CASE

The victim of a mugging picks Frank "The Hammer" Reaser out of a police line-up. Frank is well-known by the police and is reputed to know a great deal about this mugging and a host of other criminal activities such as prostitution, drugs, and illegal gambling. However, Frank has strong connections to a powerful organization, and he is released without charges being filed.

THE MYSTERY

Why is Frank allowed to go free and what organization does he work for?

CLUES

The victim had seen Frank at the scene of the crime.

Frank has cooperated with police officers before.

Frank has been in police stations many times before, but Frank has never been charged with a crime.

Police officers asked Frank to be in the line-up.

Pointing at Frank decreased the victim's credibility.

Frank's organization fights crime.

CASE 27 SOLUTION

*Frank is a police officer who
was added to the line-up.*

THE CASE

150 people sit patiently in a train station waiting for their train. Suddenly, a voice announces the train has been canceled and 147 of the people get up and leave the station. Three people remain behind.

THE MYSTERY

Why didn't the people leave the train station and in what country is the station located?

CLUES

The people heard the announcement.

The station is north of the Equator.

The three people are American.

The station is in Europe.

The station is in a country that had a famous wall torn down in 1989.

The three people speak only one language.

CASE 28 SOLUTION

The train station is in Germany and the three people don't speak German.

ABOUT THE AUTHOR

Always ahead of the game, Bob Moog's newest undertaking is truly novel. As a game inventor, his credits include such favorites as Twenty Questions® and 30 Second Mysteries®. As the CEO of University Games, he has propelled the company he founded with his college pal into an international operation that now boasts five divisions and over 350 products. Whether hosting his radio show "Games People Play," advising MBA candidates, or inventing games, Bob sees work as serious fun. He now brings his flair for fun and learning to the bookshelf with the Spinner Book line.

Enjoy Spinner Books?
Get an original game!

Find these games and more at
 or your nearest toy store.

UNIVERSITY GAMES

2030 Harrison Street, San Francisco, CA 94110
1-800-347-4818, www.ugames.com